Safe as Houses

Safe as Houses by Chris Daunt

Safe as Houses

Desmond Graham
Engravings by Chris Daunt

Belle Grove Press
2019

Published by Belle Grove Press

Text copyright 2019 Desmond Graham
Engravings copyright 2019 Chris Daunt

Design & layout by Poppy Holden

Acknowledgements

I am grateful to the editors of 'The Antigonish Review' (Canada), 'Cyphers' (Dublin) and 'Stand' (Leeds UK), where some of these poems have been previously published.

I would like to thank Alan Turnbull for sharing with me his knowledge of Chardin.

Contents

My father's phrases

The Revolution of M. Chardin

My Father's Phrases

My father's phrases

were of the people
he spoke
as other people spoke
and listened
I supposed
with measurements
in common use

the difference
was in the one
who used them
someone's 'bearing up'
was someone else's
'turned the corner'
or another's 'can't complain'

but they always
had a future
'one way
or another'
things would 'turn out

for the best'
'you wait and see'

they stayed there
rooted
to a present
where 'it can't be helped'
'made do'
'come what may'
and 'soldiered on'

as they had learnt to do
at school
filling in the spaces
left them
in their primers
for the flocks
and herds and gaggles

named
as their collectives
and the similes
which always
stayed the same
white as a sheet
and easy

as falling
off a log -
their idioms
were nothing more
or less
than what's
expected

from a book of life
with proper spellings
and neat
margins
others wrote
who knew
and told them -

we know
what happened
to the comfort
of their phrases
shared
like faces recognized
in every place they went -

we listen on
in silence
lost for words
and dumb from chatter
rightly
don't believe a word
that's said

and find the echoes
of their phrases
like choruses from songs
we long moved-on from
like times of year or seasons
which come round again
and never seem to fit

or like that banging
of a bedroom door
that gets us up again

past midnight
and we stand
then linger
far longer than expected

measuring
the scale of silence
then shut tight the door

'Safe as houses'

safe as houses
we were not
ever

as the overhead Metro
of *Dornier* and *Heinkel*
made its nightly rumble
down in the jungle
we all heard
though I was little enough
to be kept in the doll's pram
all night through

what use
the knowledge
the danger
- told later -
was all meant for others
twenty miles east
in the Docks and tenements

of London

'safe
as houses'
ours cracked
like some minor Frankenstein
some monster out of film
some worry lines
scoring the cheeks of it
from all those guns

'safe as houses'
as my father
would say
questioned after doubt
a promise for the future
the long term forecast
always there

as he was not
when he fell
in the kitchen
- or so I guessed –
receiving news
in the telegram
onto my mat

back
from his funeral
my mother
still with us
alone with the cat
who'd attacked her
once he was gone

still giving welcome
still reassuring
waiting
'safe as houses'
at a loss in her flat

'Clean as a whistle'

always a bullet
to my mind
passing straight through
and someone surviving

how all those deaths
were from wobble
or stumble
the same thing
lodged
and not gone through

like failure
bad news
missed possibility
things never got rid of
however you tried

and as for the whistle
that was the neighbours'
preoccupied
lucky
surprised to get through
never for you

'Bring the house down'

as my father hoped
on stage
each weekend
but never
quite like that

compère
comedian
Aristocrat
of Variety
the show went on

each time the house lights
lit
then dimmed
the bubbles of faces
in the front two rows
sparkled with freedom
of laughter

he could
raise the roof
perhaps
but never
bring down the house

he even drove home
quiet as a chauffeur
just in case

'A funny look'

we all had it
felt it move
through the mouth
ripple
and settle
onto each
of our features
angle our head
and stay there
instead of an answer
our way out

with a touch
of suspicion
a hint
of concurrence
an inkling
of doubt
half in
on the joke
but which joke
and whose was it
and more than half
out

if I conjured
my family
back from the dead
like the line kings
in *Macbeth*
and asked them
what was it like there

now you can tell
each one
would pause
stay silent
and give me
that funny look

'For crying out loud'

crying out loud
was what our fathers
never did
even quietly

out loud
was in silence here
and for them
and that made it worse

no tears
no sounds of a shout
no weeping
just that warning

'for crying out loud' -
and we heeded
stopped
in our tracks

we kept to the shallows
heads down
just above water

asking no questions

wished
more than anything
never
to hear

but what did it
sound like
how loud
was the loudest

and when
had they heard it -
that crying out loud -
and did they still hear

'A bundle of nerves'

they always called me
and I was puzzled

for no bundle I knew
resembled
what I felt

my nerves
wanted attention
took place on my face

took over my breathing
hitched up my trousers

gave me a cough

they held me
in hiccups of sniffing
endless in-taken breath

and between them
I talked
non-stop

with a stutter
like ems
for a printer

filling the spaces
forcing my listener
to stay

I could have exploded
without them
my bundle of nerves

my weird borealis
my fifth of November
my sailor's caul

for rough seas
through childhood
still needed in port

'Beyond a joke'

beyond a joke
I would never wish him
whose shy smile
was always available
whose natural mode
was straight ahead
with one eye to the
rear-view mirror
and his lips moving
in some song from G and S
and who listened always
for the counterpoint
and your part
late in entry
but always welcomed
me taking time
to get there
lagging with the hard notes
and he somehow
finding the breath
to be there at the finish
as I was not
and never really

so full of trust from him
I never could believe
a need was needed
though how I wish now
and - quite another question -
hope the last laugh
was somehow in his reach
though I too know
one subject

made him fearful

and he left me
with enough of humour
more than I could dream of
as I fall short now
beyond a joke

The Revolution of M. Chardin

I must forget everything I have seen so far and even the manner in which such subjects are treated by others.
                                                                    (Chardin 1730)

as if enthroned
but with no need
for pomp
a copper water urn

almost human
with its slightly bulky
waist
its rings for ears
its shoulders
its metal turban
pom-pommed
as a hat

no features
but some lineaments
of light
of shadow
cast
to give it
greater weight

instead of donors
in attendance
on one knee and small
a jug
its lid
a ladle leant against a wall

instead of altar
a stool for stand
and tin
to catch
each drop

and we take in
the nature
of this place
not godless
but with no need
of saint
not faceless
but with no need
for talk

substantial
in metal
wood
and pot
dimensioned
by the moulding fall
of light

there is no need
to touch
what we can almost

touch
as far
as that is possible
through sight

another time
a maid will come
and carry water
another time
the jug
will find its weight
perched
on a woman's
fingers
poured mid air

another time
the urn
will almost fill
the scullery
it dominates
purposeful
unmoving
in a country way
sedate

but here
meanwhile
we can stand back
or come up close
close as we like
join in
everything
is taking place

like a small cast
in a Bergman workshop
or Shakespeare's troupe
today the pot
plays Hamlet
next week
a Seville orange
will be queen

and after that
the orange
will be jester
the large pot
taken down a peg
the body
of a king

this stage
is always open
stone-shelf
back-wall
where colours
change
according to the paint

and the floor
is where we stand
watching
minutes falling
like the shucked shells
dropped
by groundlings
mouths agape

His quiet mastery overthrew the baroque still life of Holland and made
mere decorators of his contemporaries; in France nothing was able to
compete with him from the death of Watteau to the Revolution.
(André Malraux 1951)

[Liberté]

just before
the guillotine
was ever put up

after
when the best career move
was offering out your wife -
though still in fashion -

while still
a layer of scent
and more
another blast of musk

made gatherings less hazardous
but did not stop the pox

when young women
went on swings
with layered skirts
and men observed them
as they straddled seats

how grand to find
no show of wealth
no plain hypocrisy
the virtues
of having human use

of having no master
no need
yourself
in company with others
equally of use

and in the commonwealth
of a kitchen's floor
and walls
and table
free
to carry out your shape

[Egalité]

with the copper water urn
the ladle
the small pepper pot
the short-handled casserole

the woodpile
the piled planks
the collected nails
and handmade brick

with the awl
and adze
and best chisel
the dust
in the corner of the box
the small spider
running out

and the woman
in the doorway
talking to a man
we cannot see
with a child of six
who waits
or wants to come along
with the ironed apron
and grazed knee
and what will become of them

everything that has no stare
or gaze
or threat in it
and looks straight back

[Fraternité]

here is a rabbit
hung up
dead

a hook
between its back legs
and tied feet

no spear-wound
but spread belly fur
where it has waited
in the leather
of the game-bag
jolted against the side

and upside down now
as we were told
of Peter
its round head
just above the stone shelf
its front paws
in mid air
as if in flight
but stiff
its ears lifted
at no angle
of any living use

and on the table
lark and thrush
thrown down in death
almost embracing
making their own pietà
to the side

some sprigs of marjoram
stick out
beside the tied feet
and wall hook -

a plain bouquet
in full leaf

dusty
catching light
ready as a posy
for a grave

*At the age of seven or eight, they put a chalk-holder in our hand. We begin
to draw, after engravings, eyes, mouths, noses, and ears, then feet,
hands. Our back has been bent over the sketchbook for a long time when
we finally come face to face with a statue of the Hercules or with the Torso
[Belvedere] … After spending days without end and lamplit nights before
an immobile and inanimate nature, we are presented with the living
reality, and suddenly the work of all the preceding years seems to come
to nothing … One has to teach the eye to look at nature; and how many
there are who have never seen it nor ever will!*

(Chardin 1765)

a pyramid
of wild strawberries -
who holds them up

a basket of peaches
on two layers of leaves
settled forever -
if we could survive to look

a glass of wine
half full
or almost a half

not there to drink
not there to taste
not there even
to sniff for a bouquet

a knife
its handle
its blade almost out of sight

a walnut
opened
one half
removed from its shell
the other
intact
at rest

like a cradle
a hand held open
a coracle
of sorts
and none of these
at all

and three pears
Massif Central
brought within touch
each slope and summit
precipice and peak
shrunk from its distance
buffed with light
each pear solid
settled
filled with itself

it is as if Adam
naming the things
of Eden
had only paint
and named them
with that

To look at the paintings of others, it seems I need different eyes; to look at those of Chardin, I need only to make good use of those nature has given me.

(Diderot 1763)

so easy to go past
were it not necessary
to keep them safe from light

his late pastels
to be preserved in dark
like so much else

and his own way
just like his face
(three times portrayed)

so late so bright in age
half-eyeing us
above pince-nez

or gazing

straight
at the subject

of himself
or us
or in this portrait

of his second wife -
round faced
and almost looking to the side

there is no need to ask
to whom or what
she gazes

what that look means
is hers
and he knows well

for they have let us
see
together

just a little
of what they knew
each day

Chardin's Urn by Chris Daunt

This book is limited to
175 numbered copies and
12 specially bound copies
signed by the author
and by the artist

27/175